ACTIVE SCIENCE

Colourful Light

Julian Rowe and Molly Perham

W

FRANKLIN WATTS
LONDON • SYDNEY

Contents

aCtiVE SCiENCE

B48 206 2218 MSC

ROTHERHAM LIBRARY AND INFORMATION SERVICES

This edition 2004

First published in 1993 by
Franklin Watts
96 Leonard Street
London EC2A 4XD

Franklin Watts Australia
45-51 Huntley Street
Alexandria NSW 2015

Editorial planning: Serpentine Editorial
Scientific consultant: Dr. J.J.M.Rowe

Designed by the R & B Partnership
Illustrator: David Anstey
Photography: Peter Millard

Additional photographs:
Chris Fairclough Colour Library 6, 20, 30 (top and bottom);
ZEFA 16, 19 (bottom); The Hutchison Library 19 (top);
Eye Ubiquitous 29.

Dewey Decimal Classification 531
A CIP catalogue record for this book is
available from the British Library

ISBN 0 7496 5618 2

Printed in Malasyia

 SAFETY WARNING

Activities marked with this symbol require the presence and help of an adult. Plastic should always be used instead of glass.

Rainbows

Have you seen a rainbow? When the sun shines on a rainy day an arch of bright colours appears in the sky.

How many colours can you see in this rainbow?

Find a tumbler
and mirror made of
plastic, and a piece
of white paper.

Fill the tumbler with
water.
Stand the tumbler
on the white paper
near a window.

Put the mirror in the
tumbler.
Move the tumbler so
that sunlight shines
through the water
onto the mirror.

Can you see a rainbow on the white paper?

Bubbles

The sunlight that shines through the window is made up of lots of colours.

In a rainbow you can see each colour by itself. When light strikes a tiny drop of water, it splits into different colours.

Can you see rainbow colours in these bubbles?

Find some bubble mix.
Blow big and small
bubbles.
Do they all have
rainbow colours?
Where do the
colours come
from?

Blowing bubbles

Where else do you see
rainbow colours?

Coloured light

If you mix all the colours of the rainbow together you make white light.

If you mix two or more of them you make a coloured light. In this picture, different coloured lights make different coloured shadows on the wall.

Find a piece of white card, a tumbler, a pair of scissors, a sharp pencil and some crayons or paints.

Scissors

Stand the tumbler on the white card and draw round it. Ask an adult to help you cut out the circle.

Draw six equal sections on the card. Colour each one a colour of the rainbow.

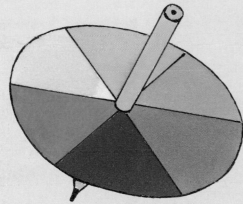

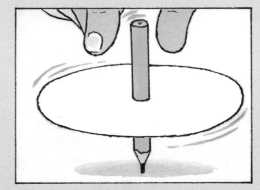

Make a hole in the middle of the card. Stick a pencil through it.

Now try spinning your colour spinner. What colour is it when it is spinning fast?

11

Mixing colours

Paints and coloured things contain pigments. Pigments take in, or absorb, some of the colours in the light. The colour you see is sent back, or reflected.

Why do you think an object looks blue, or yellow, or green?

Try mixing colours with your paints. Mixing paints is not the same as mixing coloured lights. What happens if you mix all the colours together?

Yellow and blue make green.

Red and blue make purple.

Red and yellow make orange.

Blue, red and yellow make dark brown.

Seeing colours

This paper looks green. It absorbs all the colours in the white light shining on it except the green light.

We see the green colour that is reflected into our eyes. Grass looks green because it reflects green light.

Look at the pictures these children are holding. Which train stands out best against the background?

Warning colours

Some colours are easier to see than others. Bright colours are useful warning signals.

The yellow colour of this frog warns other animals that it is poisonous. Fire engines are red so that everyone can see them clearly and get out of the way.

When you go out walking it is a good idea to wear brightly-coloured clothes. They stand out against the green and brown background of the countryside.

People will find you more easily if you get lost.

Camouflage

Birdwatchers wear dull-coloured clothes that cannot easily be seen against the bushes and trees. This disguise, or camouflage, allows them to get close to the birds without disturbing them.

Many animals have colours that match their surroundings. These colours help to camouflage the animals and protect them against enemies.

The chameleon above can change the colour of its skin to match its surroundings.

This moth on the right is not easy to see when it rests on the bark of a tree.

Travelling light

Light travels in straight lines. It does not bend around things. Look at these rays of sunlight shining through the trees.

Light travels more slowly through glass and water than it does through air. When a ray of light travels from air through water it changes direction. This makes these flower stems look broken.

Shadows

A solid object does not let light travel through it. It casts a shadow. A shadow is made where most of the light cannot reach.

Can you see which objects made
these shadows?

Bouncing back

Some materials reflect more light than others. The smooth, flat shiny surface of a mirror reflects nearly all of the light. A rough, dark surface hardly reflects any light.

See how the shoe and the four footprints are reflected in the mirror.

A shape which is exactly the same on both sides is called symmetrical. When you hold a mirror along the centre of it, you see the whole object.

What happens if you hold a mirror against each of these pictures?

Reflections

The real clock looks different from the reflection you see in the mirror.
Can you see how it is different?

The reflection is the wrong way round. The numbers have changed sides. You can't read the numbers.

What happens if you hold two mirrors at an angle in front of the clock? Now the reflection in one mirror is the right way round. Can you work out why this happens?

Funny faces

Find a big spoon and look at your reflection in it.

The back of the spoon bulges outwards. Look at your reflection in the back of the spoon. It looks small!

The bowl of the spoon is hollow. Your reflection in the bowl looks much bigger. But which way up is it?

Curved mirrors change the size and shape
of objects that are reflected in them. Mirrors
with lots of curves make very funny
reflections.

Think about...
light

This is a full moon. It looks very bright in the clear sky at night. But the moon has no light of its own. It simply reflects the light of the sun.

This child cannot see, but can still read. A blind person uses fingers to read with by touching the marks on the page.

A cat can see better in the dark than you can. Its eyes are sensitive to light you cannot see. Cats can hunt their prey in the dark.

Face the light from the window. NEVER look directly at the sun. Ask a friend to look into your eyes. Are your pupils big or small?
Then look into a dark cupboard.

What size are your pupils?

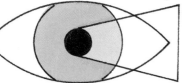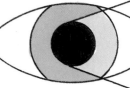

Large pupils let in more light, so you can see better.